JOBS AND PROFESSIONS

Riddles

FREE COLORING PAGES

Written by Philipa Alvarez

Jobs and Professions Riddles by Philipa Alvarez
Published by Philipa Alvarez

Cover by Philipa Alvarez
ISBN: 9788195112296
Printed in USA
First Edition

JOBS AND PROFESSIONS

Riddles

By Philipa Alvarez

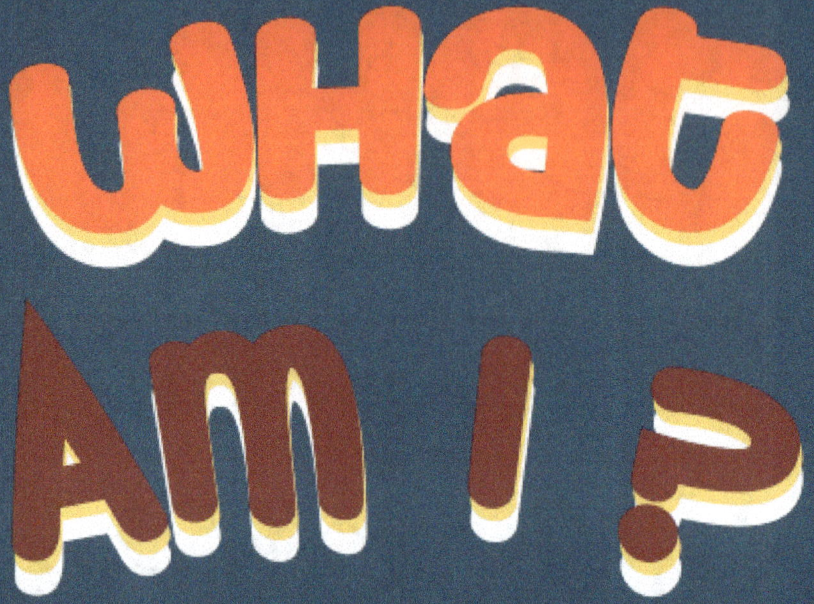

I'm a helper who wears a white coat,
To keep you healthy, that's what I devote.
I can diagnose yourills and cure your pains,
And make you feel better once again.

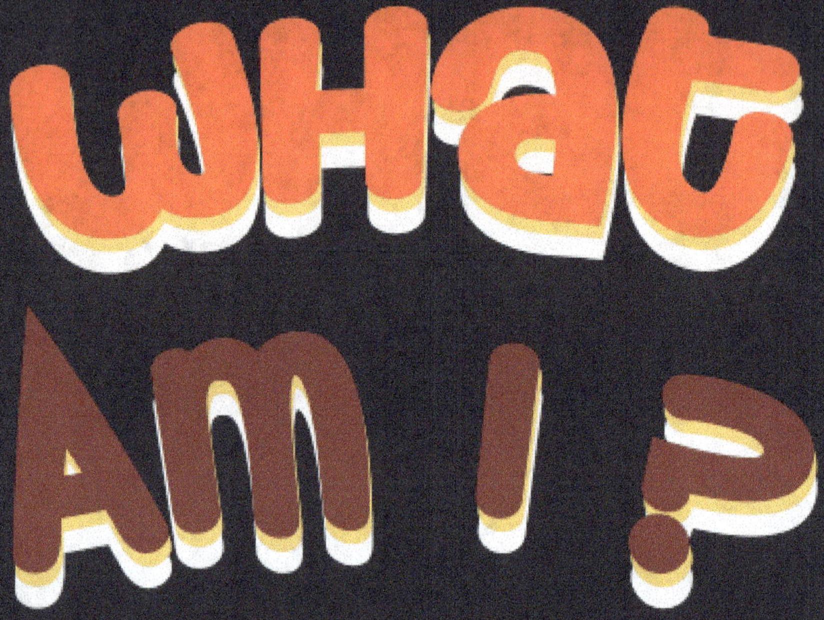

I help you read and write and spell,

And solve problems, can you tell?

I grade your work and give you praise,

And guide you through your learning phase.

WHAT AM I ?

I'm someone who battles flames
with all my might, And rescues people
when they're in fright. I use Hoses
and Pumps and tools galore,
to put out fires and save so much more.

WHAT AM I?

I chop and stir, and season just right,
And present my food with colors so bright.
I work in a kitchen, with pots and pans,
And create meals with my own hands.

WHAT AM I?

I stand up for what is right and fair,
And defend my clients with great care.
I use the law to help those in need,
And fight for justice
with diligence and speed.

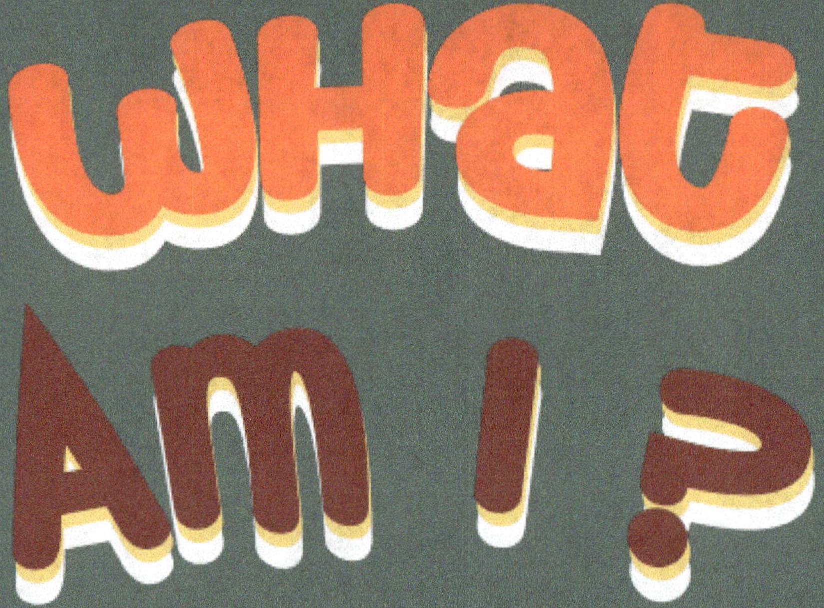

I work with creatures who bark and meow,
I help them when they're sick or have an ow.

I give them medicine and make them well,
And even listen to their tails and tell.

WHAT AM I?

I use my hands to mold and shape,
And bring to life what's in
my head, no mistake.
I make things pretty, with colors and lines,
And create artwork that really shines.

WHAT AM I?

I love to learn and explore each day,
And ask questions in my own way.
I run experiments and take notes,
And study things under microscopes.

WHAT AM I ?

I wake up with the rooster,

at the break of dawn, And

I work until the daylight is gone.

I milk the cows and gather eggs,

And store up hay in wooden pegs

WHAT AM I ?

I use a mirror and a special light,

to make your smile shiny and bright.

I use a drill and some silver fill,

And teach you how to brush with skill.

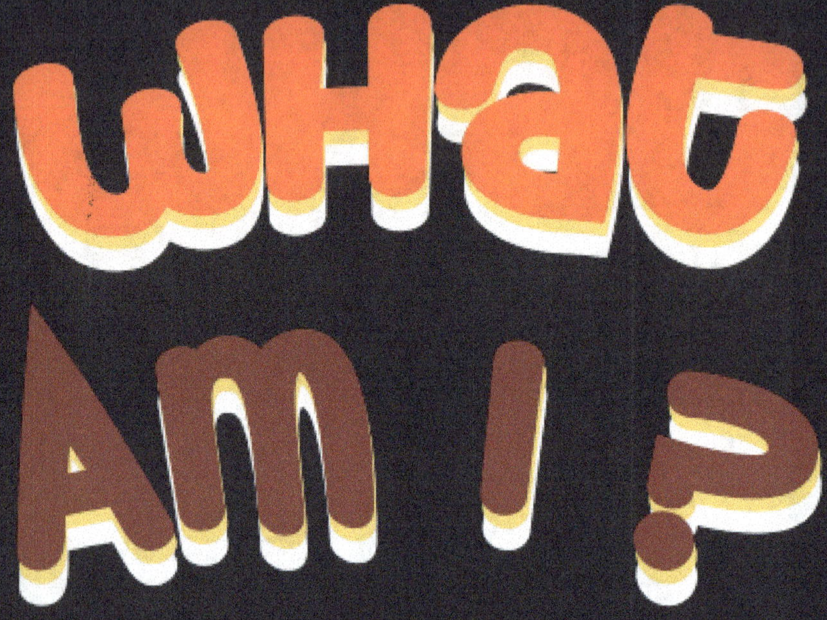

I'm someone who loves to recite lines,
And perform on stage under bright shine.
I express emotions with every move,
And tell stories that will make you groove.

I'm someone who loves to keep the peace,
And make sure everyone's worries cease.
I respond to calls from far and wide,
And help people feel safe and secure inside.

JOBS AND PROFESSIONS

Coloring Pages

By Philipa Alvarez

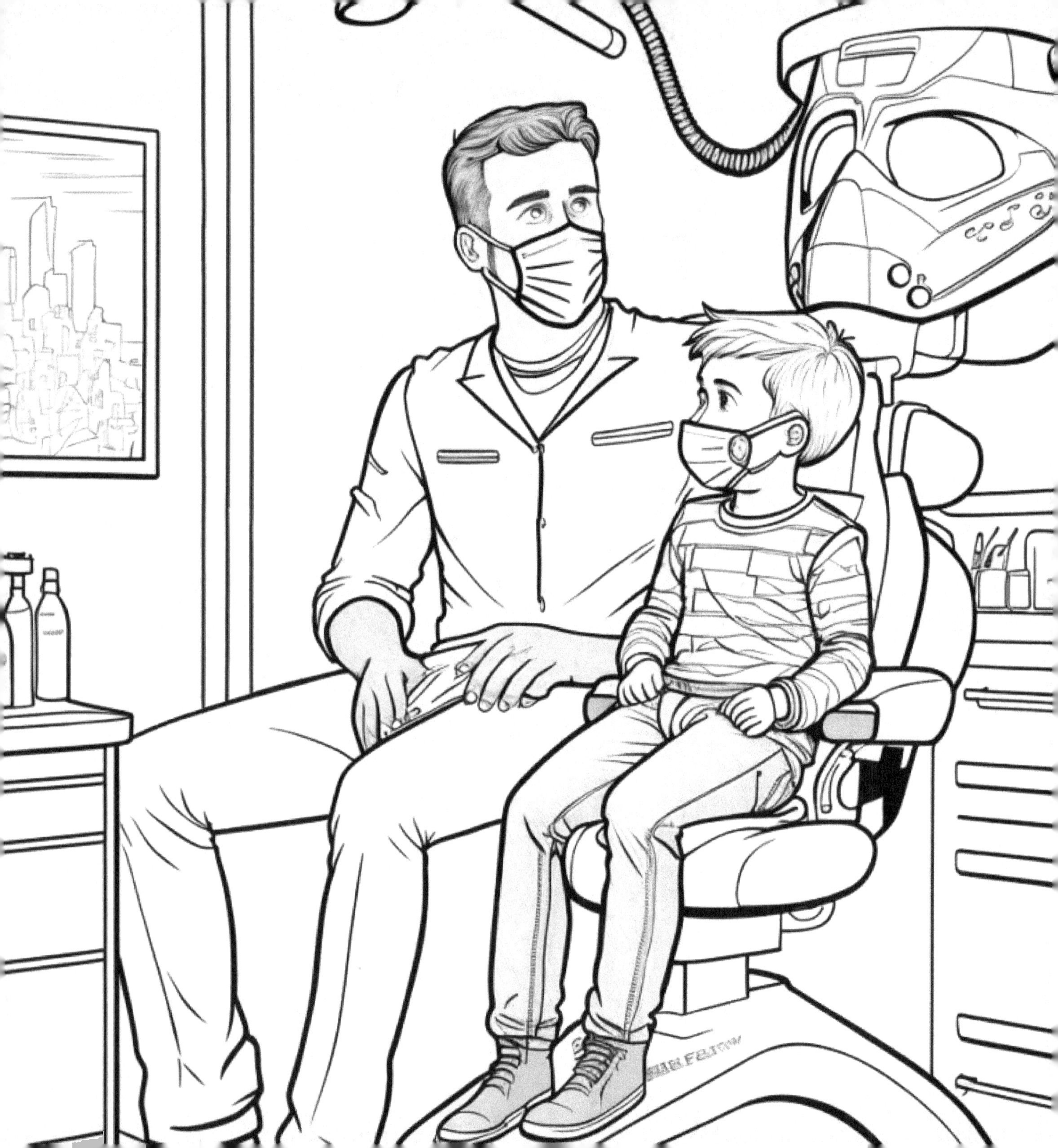

THE
END